C000183754

Deepening Faith

A Lent Study Course
on the Gospel of Mark

Tony Castle

First published in 2001 by
KEVIN MAYHEW LTD
Buxhall, Stowmarket, Suffolk IP14 3BW
Email: info@kevinmayhewltd.com

© 2001 Tony Castle

The right of Tony Castle to be identified as the author
of this work has been asserted by him in accordance with
the Copyright, Designs and Patents Act 1988.

All rights reserved. No part of this publication may be
reproduced, stored in a retrieval system, or transmitted,
in any form or by any means, electronic, mechanical,
photocopying, recording or otherwise, without the
prior written permission of the publisher.

Scripture quotations are taken from the Holy Bible,
New International Version, copyright © 1973, 1978, 1984,
by International Bible Society. Used by permission of
Hodder & Stoughton Ltd. All rights reserved.

9 8 7 6 5 4 3 2 1 0

ISBN 1 84003 837 3
Catalogue No 1500470

Cover design by Angela Selfe
Edited by Katherine Laidler
Typesetting by Louise Selfe

Printed and bound in Great Britain

Contents

Introduction

Every three minutes a Christian dies for their faith.

This is the startling claim made by Release International, in their journal *Witness*.[1]

The organisation, based in Kent, should know because it was founded on the experience of the famous Pastor Wurmbrand, who, prior to 1965, spent fourteen years in Communist prisons. It confidently states that some 164,000 Christians died for their faith in 1999. *Witness* estimates that

> more Christians have been martyred in the twentieth century – 'the century of genocide' – than in the previous 1900 years combined.

Jesus had prophesied that 'if they persecute me, they will persecute you also' (John 15:20). By the end of the first century, when John's Gospel was written, the Christian community had already suffered persecution, not only in Jerusalem but also in Rome, where Mark's Gospel is believed to have been written.

The Executive Director of Release International, Eddie Lyle, writes:

> From our contacts we are very much aware that persecution of believers is actually on the increase. It may not always make the news, but around the world, from Afghanistan to Yemen, the call to follow Christ can be a costly one.

He adds: 'There is a rare beauty that emerges in the lives of Christians who suffer, and it is in the place of deprivation that the Church most flourishes.'

In the pages that follow we are going to see how true this was in Rome, in the latter part of the first century of Christianity; how the Gospel of Mark was written against the background of persecution;

1. *Witness:* The Voice of the Persecuted Church. Release International, PO Box 54, Orpington, Kent BR5 9RT.

and how that experience deepened the faith of those early Christians. A simple reading of the Gospel of Mark, and Lenten meditation upon it, could be a good way for us, too, to deepen our faith. Mark appears to have written his Gospel for a community that was predominantly non-Jewish, going through suffering and persecution and needing to be strengthened in its faith. The Gospel is, therefore, very much a 'catechetical' or teaching document.

Throughout the last hundred years scholars have debated how historical this Gospel is and who the true author might be. A certain Papias, bishop of Hierapolis in Asia Minor, writing in the early part of the second century, identifies Mark as 'Peter's interpreter'. It was presumed – and there is some evidence to support this – that the Gospel was written in Rome, where, tradition says, Peter conducted a ministry and was executed. This would have been during the persecution waged by the Emperor Nero against the Christian community there.

Some scholars, however, have been very sceptical about Papias' testimony and the debate continued throughout the twentieth century. 'The most reasonable verdict on the theory that the author of the Gospel is John Mark is "not proven" – but not disproved either.'[1] Whoever collected together the material for this Gospel, and edited it into the shape in which we have it, the important point is that the Church from the earliest days has accepted it 'as a true testimony' which is 'entirely trustworthy'.[2]

This little book is a pastoral aid, not an academic study or commentary on Mark's Gospel. It is a simple stimulus to meditation on some themes that appear to be present in that Gospel – themes that could help us to grow in faith during Lent. There are many ways to use sacred Scripture. In his second letter to Timothy, Paul suggests three:

> All Scripture is inspired by God and useful for refuting error, for guiding people's lives and teaching them to be upright. (2 Timothy 3:16)

1. *Eerdmans Dictionary of the Bible.* William B. Eerdmans Publishing Co., Grand Rapids, Michigan.
2. *An Introduction to the New Testament.* Raymond Brown. Doubleday.

Here, the intention is that during Lent readers may find some support and encouragement for a deepening of faith, in a society which, like first-century Rome, is widely ignorant of Christianity and often hostile to the ideals and values of Christ. For, as Paul continues, 'this is how someone who is dedicated to God becomes fully equipped and ready for any good work'.

As with my previous Lenten book, *By His Wounds,* the material is divided into five chapters because it is customary to start Lenten discussion groups in the first full week of Lent and not meet in Holy Week. Ideally each participant should have their own copy of the book and read the full chapter *before* coming to the meeting. The group leader, after an introductory prayer, might like to give her/his own short summary of the chapter's content before leading the discussion, point by point. Other questions may suggest themselves to the group leader while preparing for the group meeting; that is all to the good. The more the group can adapt the material to their own needs the better.

The prayer offered is only a suggestion; the best closing prayer is that which springs spontaneously from the 'life' of the group.

All quotations from Scripture are taken from the *New International Version.*

Whether this book is used by groups or individuals, by teachers for school assemblies or pastors for sermon material, I hope that it will encourage people to give time to reading and studying the Scriptures more seriously.

Tony Castle

CHAPTER ONE

Faith in Jesus, the Christ

There is a wonderful 94-year-old lady who attends our church – always cheerful in spite of ill health, with a rock-solid faith. She and her husband, by dint of hard work and perseverance, succeeded in getting a church built in the 1960s in our large village. She is a very homely woman, well known to countless members of the parish and village, but she is always addressed as *Mrs* Collins. Her Christian name is actually Catherine, but no one feels that it is appropriate to use it.

At the time of Jesus, titles were important. It was a society, under Roman domination, where everyone knew their place. Until Jesus assumed the title of 'Rabbi', as a wandering teacher, he had no particular title. It is Mark who tells us that Jesus was a *tekton* (the Greek for woodworker or carpenter) (6:3), so he was not of the lowest order of society – a slave – or a labourer, but a lowly artisan. Later (11:3), he is known as 'the Master'. Exactly halfway through the Gospel (8:29) Jesus asks his Apostles a searching question:

Who do you say I am?

This question is as important today as it was to the people for whom Mark wrote. Was Jesus of Nazareth anyone really special, or just a gifted preacher? A gradual revelation takes place as Mark's Gospel unfolds. In a way, the answer is pre-empted in the short prologue to the Gospel, which opens with two titles for Jesus, the carpenter of Nazareth.

The beginning of the Gospel about Jesus Christ, the Son of God.

The two titles are 'the Christ' and 'the Son of God'. Before we look more closely at these titles, it is important to appreciate that the Gospel – or the 'Good News' – is going to be unveiled in the 'preaching' that follows. Likewise, the belief that Jesus is the Messiah (Hebrew version of the Greek word 'Christos', or Christ) is gradually going to be revealed, first by his friends, then a blind beggar.

Finally, the Jewish crowds come to this understanding and acknowledge that Jesus is the promised Messiah. It is not obvious to everyone from the beginning.

At the coronation of Queen Elizabeth II in 1953, the moment came for her to be anointed. For the first time in history television cameras in Westminster Abbey recorded every action. To save the embarrassment of the young queen, since the anointing with holy oil was to the upper chest, the bishops in attendance, vested in their copious robes, gathered closely round the Archbishop of Canterbury, blocking the view of every camera.

The United Kingdom's monarch is the Lord's anointed. The anointing of kings is a religious practice that stretches right back through history to Old Testament times. The prophet Samuel, on God's instruction, anointed Saul over 3000 years ago (1 Samuel 10:1). He was the first anointed King of the Israelites. So the title 'the anointed of the Lord' was used by the Jewish kings, emphasising that they had been specially chosen and set apart by God to act in his name. The title ('Messiah' = the anointed) took on a fuller and deeper meaning through the prophecies of Isaiah and Jeremiah. They spoke of the appearance, one day, of a future king of the House of David, whose rule would be glorious, wise and secure. This hope remained alive through the exile of the Jewish People in Babylon; in fact, that experience nourished it.

There were other titles, too, for this promised Messiah. One was 'King of the Jews', and another 'Son of God'. These two were connected, because if you were the king of the Jews then you were a 'son of God'. This did not suggest that the Jewish king was divine, but that God ruled his People through his appointee, or 'son'. So the Messianic title 'Son of God' does not, as it applies to the Messiah, suggest that the person is divine. Those, at the time of Jesus, who used it of him did not appreciate that he really was divine. The concept and belief that Jesus, the Christ, was really and truly divine – the second person of the Trinity – came much later, as the Christian community developed and became clearer in their understanding of exactly who and what Jesus of Nazareth was and is.

Other, more obscure, titles for the Messiah existed in the writings of the prophets, but they were not popular because they did not meet people's needs and triumphalist expectations. Two of these Messianic titles were 'Son of Man' and 'Suffering Servant'. The first can be found in the Book of Daniel and the second comes from Isaiah. It was these titles that Jesus used and applied to himself (he never actually calls himself the 'Suffering Servant' but does allude to it). He must have felt that these best described his calling and his mission.

It is Mark who introduces us to the preference Jesus has for the Messianic title 'Son of Man'. In one sentence Jesus appears to bring together his two preferred titles: 'The Son of Man himself came not to be served but to serve, and to give his life as a ransom for many' (Mark 10:45).

The important question that Jesus asked his disciples – 'Who do *you* say I am?'– prompted Peter to reply, on behalf of all the Apostles, 'You are the Christ (the Messiah).' This was clearly an important affirmation, a turning point. After months of being with him, hearing him preach and witnessing the miracles, the friends of Jesus are ready, at last, to acknowledge that he is the long-awaited and promised Messiah. The reaction of Jesus is surprising; he wants them to keep it to themselves – 'Jesus warned them not to tell anyone about him' (Mark 8:30). So the crowds were still in ignorance. No one outside the Apostolic group had yet come to the conclusion that Jesus, the good preacher and miracle-worker from Nazareth, was the Messiah.

The Jewish People were expecting the Messiah, but they were not expecting him to be divine. (Any more than now, in the twenty-first century, as the Jews still await the Messiah, do they expect that great spiritual leader, when he comes, to be divine.) They could not entertain such an expectation, because they lived, sometimes fiercely, by that summary of their faith –

> Hear, O Israel, the Lord our God is one Lord. (Deuteronomy 6:4-9)

This is the Shema, the most important Jewish prayer, repeated by every devout Jew every morning and evening. It is the first prayer he or she learns as a child and the last he is required to say at death. It is the prayer that rang out in the gas chamber at Auschwitz, as the gas drifted down from the vents above their heads. It is both the foundation stone and the keystone of Judaism. It was totally unthinkable for the Apostles and the first disciples, all of whom were devout Jews, to have any idea that God could walk this earth among them. They knew, with the certainty of their ancient faith, that the one God's presence was to be found in the sacred Devir (Holy of Holies) in the small central building of the Temple.

An interesting question is: when did Jesus himself realise that he was the Messiah? (Matthew and Luke in their Gospels show that Jesus was the Messiah from the beginning; but the question here does not query that; it asks: when did Jesus *personally realise* that he is the Messiah?) This question, it must be stressed, is open to debate, but it would appear to be answered at his Baptism by his cousin John, the Baptiser.

The Alister Hardy Research Centre, in Oxford, founded by the late Sir Alister Hardy, conducted research into the claim that some people seemed to have 'religious experiences'. After extensive research the Centre demonstrated, in the 1980s, that religious experience is widespread. Various surveys and polls conducted in England, the USA and Australia showed that 48 per cent of people replied 'yes' to the question, 'Have you ever been aware of, or influenced by, a presence or power, whether you call it God or not, which is different from your everyday self?'

From the survey it was evident that the experiences that people reported were deeply personal and are often life-changing.

At the time that I read about this research work, conducted by Dr David Hay at Oxford and Nottingham Universities, I was conducting a weekly adult class on the Synoptic Gospels. I reported the research findings to the 12 mature students and then asked if anyone present had ever had such an experience; five out of the 13 adults present claimed that they had! Only three were prepared to share those religious experiences with the group.

Jesus, in the waters of the Jordan, appears to have had such an experience. The text does not say that the crowds saw or heard anything, it was an experience personal to Jesus.

And at once, as he was coming up out of the water, he saw the heavens torn apart and the Spirit, like a dove, descending on him. And a voice came from heaven, 'You are my Son, the Beloved; my favour rests on you.' (Mark 1:10-11)

How would a devout Jew interpret these words? The title 'Son of God', as we have seen, was a Messianic title (with no divine overtones). The words 'my Son, the Beloved' carry the same meaning. Jesus would have understood that God was declaring that he, Jesus of Nazareth, was the Messiah. Perhaps stunned and finding it difficult to take in, Jesus immediately goes away, into the wilderness, to think through this awesome calling. (If the crowd had heard the words addressed to Jesus, they would have acclaimed him 'Messiah' there and then. But they don't, and it takes another three years before a crowd makes such a proclamation.)

So Mark shows Jesus, through the personal revelation at the River Jordan, coming to an understanding that *he* is the Messiah. The next revelation in the evolving story is, as we have seen, to the Apostles at Caesarea Philippi (Mark 8:27), when Jesus challenges them with the question, 'Who do you say I am?'

After the discovery and statement of belief from the Twelve, the next time a Messianic title is used, according to Mark, is when it is called out, from the roadside, by a representative of the poor and the sick. Jesus is on his final journey to Jerusalem (10:46-52) when, at Jericho, he is accosted by a blind beggar.

The religiously observant Jews, accompanying Jesus on his journey, would have dismissed this man as irreligious and unworthy of notice, on two counts: first he was very poor, and therefore not blessed by God; and he was blind, another sign (from their viewpoint) of God's disfavour. That's why the text mentions that he is sitting 'by the roadside' (he is one of the marginalised of Jewish society) and why the crowd 'scolded him and told him to keep quiet'.

Bartimaeus is not put off by their arrogance 'but he shouted all the more, "Son of David, have mercy on me."' The blind beggar uses a Messianic title to address Jesus; and no one, apart from the Apostles, had used such a title in addressing Jesus before. Notice the reply of Jesus, after he has cured him: 'Go, your faith has saved you.' The first message is clear: no matter how poor, disabled or marginalised you are, faith is the key to seeing aright. The second message is even more powerful. It is the poor and rejected man, by the roadside, who recognises who Jesus really is. Bartimaeus is the first person, after the Apostles, to recognise that Jesus of Nazareth is the Messiah.

So step by step, Mark is revealing who Jesus is; first, Jesus himself understands that he is God's 'Beloved', the Messiah. Then, after some long months together, his close friends come to the realisation that Jesus is the Messiah: 'You are the Christ', Peter says (8:29). Now we have seen that Bartimaeus, representing the marginalised of Jewish society, recognises that Jesus is 'the Son of David'. This story is immediately followed by the triumphant entry into Jerusalem and the recognition of the crowds of pilgrims entering Jerusalem for the Festival of Passover. A careful reading of Chapter 11:1-11 will show that Jesus deliberately orchestrates his very public entry into the Holy City. In these his final few days, he draws people's attention to the Messianic prophecy of Zechariah:

> Rejoice greatly, O Daughter of Zion!
> Shout, Daughter of Jerusalem!
> See, your king comes to you,
> righteous and having salvation,
> gentle and riding on a donkey,
> on a colt, the foal of a donkey.   (Zechariah 9:9)

The crowds respond by calling out Messianic slogans – 'Blessed is the coming kingdom of our father, David', and so on. At last the Jewish crowds recognise and accept Jesus as the Messiah.

The gradual revelation is now complete; from the personal discovery of Jesus, through the recognition by the Apostles, followed by that of the first individual, blind Bartimaeus, and, at last, as the end approaches, the crowds acknowledge Jesus as the Messiah. Not once, in Mark, does Jesus claim to be divine or is he acknowledged to be divine. (That is not to say that by the time he came to write, Mark had not come to believe Jesus was the divine 'Son of God'. That Messianic title had taken on a fuller and deeper meaning by the time Mark uses it in his opening statement, over 30 years after the events that he records.)

Questions for discussion

1. Do you think that the use of titles still has a place in the twenty-first century, when so many people seem to prefer addressing everyone by their first given name? Does using a title show respect or just identify a distance between people?

2. Have you ever heard or thought about the Messianic titles (e.g. King of the Jews, Son of God, etc.) of Christ before? Does a better understanding of those traditional titles help or hinder us when thinking about the role of Jesus and his redeeming work? Why do you think Jesus preferred to use the title 'Son of Man'?

3. Have you had any difficulty with the idea that, according to Mark, Jesus had to discover that he was the Messiah? Does this 'human discovery' and emphasis upon his humanity limit in any way his divinity?

4. What message is there for us in the fact that it was a marginalised person – 'sitting by the roadside' of life, poor and blind – who was the first (after the Apostles) to recognise the Messiah? Could anyone, in the group, make a link with the nativity story, found in Luke's Gospel?

5. 'Who do you say that I am?' Jesus asked his friends. Who do *we* say he is? Who do our neighbours and our non-Christian colleagues at work say Christ is? Which of the Messianic titles would mean the most to them?

6. Jesus never explicitly called himself 'The Suffering Servant', but he suggested it on several occasions. It has been said that this title is the most meaningful for our times. What do you think?

Prayer

Lord, with Peter we can say, 'You are the Christ';
 you are our Messiah, the anointed one.
We thank you for the gift of faith
 which enables us to recognise you
 not only as the promised Messiah,
 but as the divine Son of God,
 co-eternal with the Father.
May those who cannot answer your question
 'Who do you say I am?'
 one day come to recognise and accept you;
 and, with us, come to love and serve you.
Amen.

CHAPTER TWO

The testing of faith

Several years ago I had a most memorable week in Cracow, Poland. One afternoon, with time on my hands, I wandered into the narrow streets of the old city and found myself outside the door of a small, quaint-looking church. Stepping first into the dark porch and then the brightly lit nave, I immediately whipped out my camera, because right before me, dominating the left-hand side of the church, was the most amazing pulpit I had ever seen. It was an intricately constructed model of a fishing boat, or rather the prow and one side of the boat. The timbers of the hull were clearly shown, with nets hanging over the side, and there was a mast with a rolled-up sail. It was beautifully executed. Peter's fishing boat reproduced in brass. Practically, it must have been a church cleaner's nightmare; but just to see it was a lesson in itself. Clearly the architect had in mind what Jesus did in Mark 4:1. Like Christ, the preacher would proclaim the Gospel from the prow of a fishing boat.

During his preaching ministry in Galilee, Jesus chose as his base or headquarters the small lakeside, fishermen's town of Capernaum. It remains today, along with the shores of Lake Galilee, one of the few places in Israel where you can feel very close to the historical Jesus. The Franciscans, who have care of the site, confidently claim to have found the very house of Simon Peter, where Jesus lodged. A visitor can see a large part of the excavated town with its tiny houses with walls of black basalt rock (the inhabitants must have plastered over them and then whitewashed them). Beneath the existing ruins of a third-century synagogue can clearly be seen the foundations of an earlier synagogue, most probably the one referred to in Mark 1:21. From this town Jesus went out to proclaim the Gospel to the neighbouring towns and villages.

The Greek word *euaggelion* (gospel) is rarely found in any Greek literature before it is used by the early Christians; and where it is used it means 'good tidings'. For Christians it comes to mean the whole of the Christian message, and the messenger; for Christ himself, with the whole of his teaching and his death and resurrection, is God's Good News to humanity. The proof of the word's importance can be seen in its use, 72 times in the New Testament; 54 of these in Paul's letters.

The Gospel according to St Mark. Strictly speaking we do not have four Gospels; there is only one Good News, with four different accounts of it. Mark's account was not written to be read; that is, read by individuals. It couldn't be, because there would have been few in the community who could read Greek and only one or two copies of the text would have been available. No, it was intended to be proclaimed and read publicly – and, perhaps, as a whole (it takes a little over an hour). It was written to be a teaching book, to deepen and strengthen the faith of individual Christians and the community as a whole.

A 'Gospel' is a unique form of literature. Most people are under the impression that it is a life of Christ. A reading of Mark's Gospel shows that it cannot be, because so much is missing. In Mark, Jesus appears on the scene as a 30-year-old man; there is no mention of any part of his life before that. We glean nothing of his birth, childhood and early manhood from Mark. There is no description of him and no mention of any family life. You cannot write a 'life' which only covers three years: the years of his public ministry. Clearly Mark had no intention of writing a life of Christ. He was writing a teaching document that would confirm and strengthen the faith of the members of his local community.

Storms, thunder and lightning are symbolically used to good effect in many television films and dramas. How many fictitious horror stories, for example, take place on bright, sunny days? Yet real life 'horrors' – like the massacre of the children at Dunblane – do occur in ordinary weather conditions.

The Lake of Galilee is some 600 feet below sea level. When I went with a small group of teachers to the Holy Land (my second visit), I remember our minibus driver halting by a large roadside sign which was white with a blue wavy line across the centre. It read: 'This line represents sea-level.' Ahead, and far below us, stretched out in the sunlight was one of the most famous lakes in the world, set against the silhouette of the hills known as the Golan Heights. That afternoon, on the beach by Tabgha, where Simon's boat had probably been drawn up and where the feeding of the five thousand is traditionally commemorated, our small group planned to have a Eucharist. As the sacred vessels and linen were being set out on a large flat-topped rock, used as an altar, the wind got up. It was so strong by the time our Eucharist began that we had to leave our seats and stand in a tight circle, shoulder to shoulder, around the altar to prevent everything being blown away. The waters of the lake were whipped up by the wind and the fishermen, whom we had earlier seen out fishing, had all come in. Our guide told us that this was a frequent occurrence in the afternoon.

Mark tells (4:35-41) of a storm blowing up one evening as Jesus and his friends were crossing that lake: 'the waves broke over the boat, so that it was nearly swamped.' Horror! It must have been a massive storm to terrify experienced fishermen. Jesus, however, is fast asleep in the stern! 'Teacher, don't you care if we drown?' After he had quietened the storm, Jesus is not sympathetic; he turns on them and says, 'Why are you so afraid? Do you still have no faith?'

Here we can clearly see Mark's intention and the purpose of his Gospel. Notice where this story comes. There are only nine parables recorded in Mark and five of them come immediately before this story. A parable, of course, is a teaching story. So is this, like the parables, a teaching story? It certainly looks like it. That is not to say that there was no storm; on the contrary, Mark uses an event recorded in the memory of the community to teach about the importance of faith: having faith and trust in the person of Christ and his abiding presence in the community.

At the time of the Great Fire of Rome (AD 64) and Nero's persecution of the Roman Christian community, Peter, tradition tells us, was known as 'the Big Fisherman'.

The community was known as 'the barque (fishing boat) of Peter'. At his call to be a disciple, Jesus had said, 'I will make you fishers of men' (Mark 1:18). So, in AD 64, when three of Rome's 14 districts were completely destroyed by fire, Nero unleashed a vicious storm of violence against the Christian community; Peter's barque was rocked and almost swamped. The Roman Christians, who had been blamed for the fire, must have cried out in terror, as family and friends were rounded up and tortured: 'Where is Christ? Does he sleep that he does not come to our aid'; 'Master, don't you care?' Their new-found faith was sorely tested.

Through this story Mark says to the community, 'Quiet now! Be calm! Have faith and trust in Christ's presence; Jesus may seem to sleep, but he is with you; hold on, and all will be well.' After the storm will come a great calm; after death, the resurrection. It was a great and terrible testing time for the community; but it held on, in faith. It not only survived but flourished, for 2000 years.

Questions for discussion

1. It is acknowledged that Mark wrote the first Gospel, a new and unique form of literature. If Mark had not written the Gospel (copied by Matthew and Luke), do you think another follower would have 'invented' this type of Christian literature?

2. Before reading this book did you think of a gospel as a life of Christ? Can you see now how it is more valuable to us as a document written to deepen our faith in Christ?

3. Has anyone in the group had the experience of reading the whole of Mark's Gospel at one time? What benefits are there from such an experience?

4. What do we mean by saying that Christ is himself the Good News from God? As modern disciples of Christ, do we follow a teaching or a person?

5. The story of the storm on the lake was applied to the persecution of the Roman community and its need to hold on in faith. How can the story be applied to each one of us, as individuals?

6. Have you had a personal insight from this reading, or discussion, that you would like to share with the rest of the group?

Prayer

Lord Jesus, our Good News from the Father,
   your words and actions lead us to know the Father.
May we treasure your continual presence among us
   for, without you, we can know little of God.
Without you, our light and the calmer of our storms,
   we are left in the darkness and turbulence of this world's values.
Even when you appear to be silent and asleep,
   may we have a deep faith
   in your abiding presence with us and love for us.
Amen.

CHAPTER THREE

Growth in faith

The terms 'Iron Curtain' and 'Cold War' seem very dated now that Communism has lost its stranglehold on Eastern Europe. The threat and fear of the evil empire of atheistic Communism is a spectre of the past. However, when I journeyed to Poland in 1980, although we did not realise then that the end was nigh, the Iron Curtain, with all its limitations on freedom, was still fearfully in place.

A day or two before departure, I discovered that the friends of an acquaintance who were to accommodate me had not heard of my trip! On the Polish LOT aircraft taking off from Gatwick, I noticed that there were no men with the women and children who were returning, apparently after holidaying in England. (I later learnt that husbands and fathers were not allowed to leave with the rest of the family – to ensure that the women and children returned!) As the LOT aircraft came in to land at the lush green, secluded airstrip, passing the Soviet MiG fighters under camouflage nets, and taxied up to the minuscule Cracow air terminal, I was filled with anxiety. Would there be anyone there to meet me? With not one word of Polish to fall back on, I sought out for advice, in the slow-moving queue for Immigration, an elderly Polish priest who was clearly proficient in English.

The Immigration controller, who spoke as much English as I did Polish, took mysterious exception to some detail in my papers and handed me over to a huge bearded green-clad Customs man. With the aid of sign language I was instructed to empty out every item of my luggage. The subsequent intensive and leisurely search would have found the proverbial needle in the haystack – had there been one there! I was next ordered into a private room for a body search, and every pocket was emptied. I was amazed to witness the careful scrutiny of an old Southend Transport bus ticket, discovered in the top pocket of my blazer – no doubt looking for secret coded messages!

At last I was left alone with my fears. All the other passengers had long since departed, with the exception of the elderly priest whom I spied in an adjoining room receiving similar treatment. After about twenty minutes or so, my papers were thrust at me and I was dismissed with a sweep of the hand. Thankfully there were two Polish priests waiting patiently to greet me once I escaped to the terminal lounge. That night I could hardly sleep for nightmarish dreams, and throughout the first few days of my stay in Poland I kept imagining that I was being watched. Perhaps I was!

Entering the realm of Communist influence and power there was no welcome, only the climate of suspicion, fear and intimidation. Contrast this with the kingdom of God. Mark is really the first to introduce us to this phrase 'the kingdom of God' (Matthew uses as an equivalent 'the kingdom of heaven'). Most of Paul's letters were written before Mark wrote his Gospel, but Paul makes only a few passing references to the phrase.

What then is this 'kingdom of God'? This is not as simple a question as it looks. First, what it is not: it is not a place like Poland or the United Kingdom. Mark's first use of the word suggests that it is something other than a place: 'the kingdom of God is near' (1:15). The word 'kingdom' would be more easily understood if it were replaced by 'kingship'. It is about the kingship, or ruling, of God.

At the time of Jesus there were dozens of kingdoms in that part of the world; being ruled by a monarch (under the auspices of the Roman Emperor, of course) was the only known political system. Today everything is round the other way; absolute monarchs are a thing of the past and even the constitutional variety is rare.

It was natural in Israel for the religious leaders to use the image of 'king' to evoke the power of God. For Israel, God is the sole king, and the earthly king is only his representative. The prophets foretold that God would show himself as king and establish his kingdom through the agency of his Messiah. It was to be a kingdom where there would be liberty and justice, especially for the poor.

The spirit of the Sovereign Lord is on me,
because the Lord has *anointed* me,
to preach *good news* to the poor.
He has sent me to bind up the broken-hearted,
to proclaim freedom for captives.
(Isaiah 61:1)

Notice the words that I have placed in italics: 'the anointed' = 'the Messiah' and 'good news' = 'gospel'.

Using Mark's Gospel as the foundation for his own, Luke actually sets out the above text from Isaiah and uses it as Jesus' manifesto (or programme) as the Messiah.

Like many other Jews of his time, Jesus was expecting God to act decisively and dramatically in history; to inaugurate a new age. God was going to become King, at last, in a new way; in a way that he had promised through the prophets. After long years of oppression, God would come to Israel, would reign as King. When Jesus speaks of 'the kingdom of God' he is not talking about a place up in the skies, or a future 'Church'; he is thinking of this present world, particularly Israel, being ruled the way God wanted it to be. Jesus taught us to pray that the kingdom would come on earth, as in heaven.

How did a person 'enter' this 'kingdom of God'? Remembering that it is not a place but 'God ruling', it is about accepting God as 'king' or 'leader' in one's life. In modern terms we would call it: seeking God's will and trying faithfully to live by it. The community of those who try to live by the Messiah's programme and accept him as Lord and Christ (Acts 2:36) promotes the values of 'God ruling', and, in a sense, becomes the community of the kingdom; the Church. They say the Lord's Prayer which not only prays that everyone will accept God ruling in their lives, but says how it can be done; by doing as God asks.

Your kingdom come, your will be done.

If we do God's will, or at least try to do God's will, his 'ruling', or his kingdom, will come in our lives and, through us, in society. God can only break into our society and culture through us.

There are very few parables in Mark, compared with Matthew and Luke. Mark has only nine, compared with 24 in Matthew and 28 in Luke. In comparison there are as many miracles (20 recorded) in Mark as in the other Synoptic Gospels. Mark reports that there were many more parables told by Jesus than the ones that he chooses to record:

> . . . with many similar parables Jesus spoke the word to them . . . He did not say anything to them without using a parable. (Mark 4:33)

The parables, like the miracles, are in the text to illustrate the Good News. The five parables gathered together by Mark in chapter 4 all illustrate the central core of Jesus' preaching about the kingdom of God. However, I would suggest that the reason Mark has selected these particular parables is that they contain a special message for his persecuted people.

Once again imagine, if you will, that you are in first-century Rome, in a congregation gathered in hiding for fear of arrest, torture and execution, for being a follower of the Christ. 'Listen' to the parables:

Parable of the lamp (4:21-23)
Shine! Just as a lamp is useless if it is 'under a bowl or a bed', so you too must have the courage to 'shine' by your witness if you are arrested. Be proud of your faith in Christ, that others may see and admire your example.

Parable of the measure (4:24-25)
Give your life generously! 'With the measure you use, it will be measured to you – and even more'; if you trustingly place your life into God's hands, he will more than amply reward you in the afterlife.

Parable of the seed (4:26-29)
Grow in faith! You will not see or be able to measure your faith and trust in God. God will not ask more of you than you can bear; only when you are ready will God ask you to face pain and suffering. 'As soon as the grain is ripe he puts the sickle to it, because the harvest has come.'

Parable of mustard seed (4:30-34)

Grow in faith! You may feel that your faith is not big enough to endure what may come; keep trusting in God, and your faith will grow from 'the smallest seed' into 'the largest of all garden plants'.

Organisations, like Baroness Cox's Christian Solidarity Worldwide, Release International (already referred to) and Aid to the Church in Need keep the plight of persecuted Christians before us, so that we may not only be informed but also feel and express real solidarity with them. We really have no need to imagine persecuted Roman Christians at the time of Mark, or the tens of thousands who died in the Soviet purges of the 1920s and 1930s, when there are thousands of Christ's disciples suffering today.

However, to be faithful to Christ and the kingdom, we, in our society and culture, must do all we can to 'shine' and 'grow' as the parables suggest, for they are also addressed to us. By being proud of our faith in Christ – not hiding it for fear of mockery or ridicule – and trying to set a good example, by living generously for others, by placing all our trust in God, especially when faced with pain, rejection and setbacks, our faith will grow (unnoticed by us) into 'the largest of all garden plants' and give glory to Christ our King.

This brings us full circle back to the Garden of Gethsemane (14:36) and Christ's agony and prayer there. Jesus pleaded, as today many of his persecuted friends must do, 'Take this cup of suffering away from me' – such a human heartfelt cry. He realises, and then accepts, that this is his Father's will. God's kingdom comes (God rules in our lives) if we accept and faithfully do his will. Jesus, the Messiah, accepts his Father's will; the kingdom comes, in all its perfection, in his life. God has acted decisively and dramatically in the Gethsemane event, in and through his Son. By following each day the example of Christ's surrender, we will grow in faith and in membership of the kingdom. Above the cross, on the morrow, will be the words 'Jesus of Nazareth, King of the Jews'; Christ is forever our king, and, as he told Pilate (John 18:36), his kingdom is not of this world.

Questions for discussion

1. Do you think that people today find it more difficult to understand the term 'the kingdom of God' than the people of first-century Palestine?

2. Why did Jesus use parables when speaking of the kingdom and not just explain what he meant? Is there still a place for the use of 'parable' by preachers today?

3. When we say that Jesus was the embodiment of the kingdom, what do we mean? Is this different from saying that Jesus is the Good News?

4. Sometimes people today speak of 'kingdom values'. What are they referring to?

5. What comfort, if any, might persecuted Christians around the world today receive from the parables in Mark's Gospel?

6. We read that 'the teaching of Jesus made a great impression on them'. Why does it not make a great impression on people of the twenty-first century? Which is at fault: the message or the messengers?

Prayer

Say together, slowly and meditatively – phrase by phrase – the Lord's Prayer.

or

O Lord, you have warned us
    that you will require much of those to whom much is given.
Grant that we, who have received so much,
    may strive together, by our prayers, hard work and gifts,
    to extend to those who know you not
    what we so richly enjoy.
So may your will be fulfilled
    with the salvation of all humankind.

(Fifth-century prayer)

CHAPTER FOUR

The cost of discipleship

Late one evening, rather a long time ago in my teens, prompted by sheer nosiness, I did something rather underhand. I was home from college for Christmas. My mother and father had gone to bed, leaving me to watch a film on television downstairs. When it eventually finished I went up to my bedroom. On the way I noticed that a light still showed under my parents' bedroom door and, hearing the mutter of voices, I decided to creep along the passageway and eavesdrop! When I arrived silently at their bedroom door I bent my head to listen. After listening for a few moments I tiptoed away in embarrassment; and I still vividly remember the experience over forty years later. I learnt something that I had never known before. My mum and dad were praying together.

There's an intriguing little 'eavesdropping' recorded in Mark's Gospel (14:51-52) when Jesus is praying in the Garden of Gethsemane. After Jesus had been arrested and all his friends had fled, the armed group sent by the chief priests find and seize hold of a young man who had been lurking in the darkness. He escaped their clutches by slipping out of the loose linen garment draped around him. This event is not found in any other Gospel and seems to have no meaning or purpose in being mentioned, unless the nosey young man eavesdropping on Jesus is, as some scholars suggest, John Mark, the author of the Gospel. (Other scholars just find the event very enigmatic!)

If this is the explanation, then it answers an interesting problem. If Jesus prayed alone, apart from his sleeping disciples, how does the Gospel-writer know what Jesus said to his Father in prayer? Jesus could not have told him, or anyone else, because immediately after his agonising prayer to be spared the pain and the death of the cross, Jesus is arrested. There was no opportunity, even if Jesus had wanted to share such a private prayer, to tell a friend. The problem would appear to be solved, if John Mark knew what

Jesus was saying in prayer because he had been eavesdropping in the darkness of the shrubbery.

From my eavesdropping I learnt something that I had not known; that my parents said night prayers together. The memory has stayed with me and inspired me more than once. John Mark may have learnt something that night which stayed with him for ever. He had discovered how the Master feared death, how human he was, and equally how heroic he was in accepting his Father's will. It is no wonder, then, that the humanity of Christ comes across so strongly in Mark's Gospel; that Mark's theology is the theology of the Cross – its cost and its meaning.

The incident in the Garden also shows how human the disciples were, not that Mark was ever one of the special twelve disciples known as Apostles. John Mark is never mentioned by name in any of the Gospels. He is first named in Acts (12:12) when Peter, after his escape from prison in Jerusalem, takes refuge at 'the house of Mary, the mother of John, also called Mark'. This Jerusalem family must have been rich because their house was large enough to accommodate the local church community.

The early Christian writers, Irenaeus and Eusebius, trusted and used the writings of a certain Papias, a bishop of Hierapolis, in Asia Minor. He wrote about AD 120 and states that Mark, having become an interpreter of Peter, set down accurately, though not in order, everything that he remembered of the words and actions of the Lord. The word 'interpreter' has been understood, in our times, to mean secretary to St Peter. Since Mark was accompanying Peter and hearing his daily preaching, it has been concluded that the Gospel of Mark largely reflects the preaching of Peter, arranged and shaped by John Mark.

If you take a look at chapter 14 you will see how Mark interrupts the flow of the story of Jesus brought to trial (verses 27-31 and 66-72); there is inserted the very personal and painful account of Peter's denial of Jesus. It is not difficult to imagine that Peter, having to live with the memory of that betrayal of the Master, constantly retold his story of shame.

There is no certainty about the following, but it is commonly believed that Mark wrote down, in his own order, the preaching of Peter, following the great fire of Rome. The Roman historian Cornelius Tacitus (*c.* 55-120), writing in his *Annals*, tells how the Emperor Nero made the Christians scapegoats for the Great Fire of AD 64 (when he was probably the instigator himself to clear sites for his building plans). Tacitus believed that it was a false charge but describes how Christians were thrown to the wild dogs, crucified or burnt alive in Nero's garden. In the ferocious persecution that followed, Peter was arrested and crucified on Vatican Hill, and the Roman communities (there were several, according to Dr Eamon Duffy in *Saints and Sinners*) were left leaderless. More worrying for the Christians who survived was that now there was no apostle among them, no direct link with Christ and his teaching. Until now they had relied upon personal witness and teaching. It would be more difficult to rely upon oral tradition, so writing the teaching down became a priority. So, it is believed, Mark, who knew Peter's preaching well, settled down to record it.

There's a certain black humour in the story, dating from the 1950s, of the Englishman, the Frenchman and the Russian who, in conversation, were trying to define happiness. 'True happiness,' said the Englishman, 'is when you return home tired after work and find a gin and tonic waiting for you.' 'You English have no romance,' countered the Frenchman. 'True happiness is when you go on a business trip, find a pretty girl who entertains you, and then you part without regrets.' 'You are both wrong,' concluded the Russian. 'Real happiness is when you are in bed at four o'clock in the morning and there is a hammering at your front door, and there stand members of the Secret Police, who say to you, "Ivan Ivanovitch, you are under arrest", and you are able to reply, "Sorry, Ivan Ivanovitch lives next door!"'

What horror lies behind the humour of that story! Stalin, through his purges, disposed of many more innocent people than Hitler. Mark would have understood the hammering on the door in the night, for it was against this background – of night raids by the security forces of his day, arrests, torture and cruel death – that he wrote his Gospel. Another of Mark's themes is *discipleship* and the cost of discipleship.

Mark knew all about the cost of discipleship. He was faithful all his life, from his teens to his death. He may well have witnessed, in the Garden, the cost to Jesus of his total self-giving, and he knew that discipleship, likewise, demanded total giving. Mark records for us, in Chapter 12 (41-44) the inspiring example of the poor widow, who gave all she had to God. As Mark was writing down this very story, he would have been aware of the price being paid, by the members of his own community, for being a faithful disciple of Christ.

Imagine that you are sitting with a group of these Christians at some secret address in Rome, gathered, after dark, to celebrate the Eucharist. All the talk, as the group comes together, is of the latest arrests and executions. Some friends from your community, and perhaps members of your own family, have already been tortured and hideously killed. The elder leading the group produces a scroll and says, 'I have here an account of the Good News written for us by Brother Mark. He instructs me to read it to you.' Then you hear these words, the words, Mark says, of Jesus himself (8:34-38):

> If anyone would come after me, he must deny himself and take up his cross and follow me. For whoever wants to save his life will lose it, but whoever loses his life for me and for the gospel will save it.

And those Christians were severely tempted to save their lives (as you and I would be) by renouncing Christ and his message. It is not hard to imagine the homily which would follow: remember, the preacher would remind them, how Jesus feared death in the Garden of Gethsemane; how he was faithful to what God asked and how the resurrection followed.

Within the first 20 verses of the Gospel, Mark has Jesus calling disciples to follow him. The Gospel eventually concludes with 'go, tell the disciples and Peter' (that the tomb is empty). And the very final words are of the women disciples who 'said nothing to anyone, because they were afraid'. This Gospel really spoke to the needs of Mark's persecuted community.

Questions for discussion

1. Have you ever had a single, perhaps unexpected, experience that has changed or markedly altered your thinking, or your way of life?

2. Do you find the story (Mark 14:32-52) of Christ's prayer and arrest in the Garden disturbing or encouraging? Or perhaps both?

3. Do you think that Jesus, in the Garden of Gethsemane, could have got up, left his praying and slipped away in the dark of the night, and returned to his original home and job in Nazareth? Was he free to do that?

4. Do you know anyone, like the widow in the Gospel, who has a remarkably deep and trusting faith? Does that give their lives any particular purpose or direction? What might we learn from such people?

5. How important do you think the events in the Garden are: *not important/quite important/very important/vital* to an understanding of what follows?

6. Do you know of any places in the world today where Christians are enduring similar persecution to the Roman community at the time of Mark? Is there anything that we can do to help them?

Prayer

Lord Jesus,
    lead us to the Father.
Lead us by the example of your obedience
    to the Father's will.
Lead us by the example
    of your heroic acceptance of betrayal and denial;
    rejection and abandonment.
Lead us by the example of your total self-sacrifice,
    even to death on the cross.
May we never deny knowing you.
May we never tire of serving others,
    as you served them.
Lead us to the glory of the resurrection.
Lord Jesus,
    lead us to the Father.
Amen.

CHAPTER FIVE

The reward of faith

The burly police sergeant was looking through the letterbox in the centre of the green front door, as I pulled up in my VW Beetle. We were in Elstree Gardens, Abbey Wood, and I was responding to a phone call from a parishioner who lived opposite the home of old Mr Stevens. It was nearly 2pm and because the curtains were still drawn and the next-door neighbour had reported the smell of gas, the police and the parish office had been alerted.

In his seventies, Mr Stevens lived alone, rejected for some unknown reason by his family; his wife, to whom he was devoted, suffered from an advanced stage of Alzheimer's and was cared for in a home.

The powerfully built policeman was putting his shoulder to the door as I joined him; with a splintering sound the door gave way and out drifted the gas. We both managed to find handkerchiefs and plunged into the darkened, gas-filled passageway leading to the kitchen and the rear of the house. The police officer drew back some heavy curtains and attempted to open the window. I found the back door, drew back two bolts and threw it open. Immediately behind me was a gas cooker with two rings full on. Having turned these off, I stepped back into the back room, presumably the dining room, to find the policeman down on one knee turning off the tap to the gas fire. We still had not spoken to one another, and I never did know his name. 'Where's the old man?' he asked. At that moment I noticed what I first mistook to be a pile of dark clothes on the floor between a dining table and the wall. A step closer and I saw it was the crumpled body of Mr Stevens. We had seen the body at the same time and the policeman said, 'Look for a suicide note.' While I did that, he was radioing for a police surgeon to attend the scene. We stepped outside for some fresh air. 'Clear case of suicide,' declared the police officer. We returned to search again for the suicide note and were unsuccessful.

Shortly afterwards the police surgeon arrived; a doctor known locally for her abrupt and direct manner. I was in the dining room when she stepped over and took a look at the body. 'Heart attack,' she declared. The sergeant reported the gas-filled room (now clear) but Dr Quinn snorted and said, 'It's obvious, isn't it? The poor man came in, it was cold last evening. He had a bit of a turn, couldn't see properly, thought he'd lit the gas fire and he hadn't; went to make a cup of tea, same happened. Sat down at the table; had another attack and collapsed on the floor. No note, is there?' The policeman confirmed that there wasn't one. 'That's it, then,' said the doctor. I am sure the policeman must have felt foolish, because I certainly did. We had both completely misread the signs. What appeared to have happened had not happened!

When Jesus died everyone misread the signs. It was a stark reality; there were no choirs of angels. It appeared to be just another Roman execution, of yet another political troublemaker. Rejected and alone, the victim of religious jealousy and hatred, the abject, abandoned figure on the cross appeared to be a total failure. Mark brings out the ordinariness and the drama; only in retrospect is that dismal scene invested with unique meaning and glorious purpose.

The Passion story in Mark occupies one third of the whole Gospel; it is proportionally bigger than the space given by the other evangelists. It is a tale of broken promises, betrayal, denial, abandonment, rejection and a lonely, brutal death. But it is presented by Mark as a lesson in faith and hope – faith lesson for us all.

Holy Week, as we celebrate it, commences with Palm Sunday and the recollection of Jesus' triumphant entry into Jerusalem. On that day (Mark 11:1-11) Jesus was given superstar treatment; it was, after three years of preaching, his moment of glory, of public acknowledgement. But after that, and from that day on, everything fell apart.

Mark locates the Passover on the Thursday and says 'two days before the Passover' (14:1ff) 'the chief priests and the teachers of the law were looking for some sly way to arrest Jesus'. So when Judas approaches them 'to betray Jesus to them', they were delighted. At the Passover supper Jesus says, '. . . one of you will betray me'(14:18). And Judas does!

When Jesus foretells, 'You will all fall away' (14:27), Peter promises, 'Even if all fall away, I will not.' Jesus said to him, 'I tell you the truth . . . today – yes, tonight – before the cock crows twice, you yourself will disown me three times.' And Peter breaks his promise!

Then, in the Garden, the disciples sleep while Jesus prays to be spared the painful death that lies ahead. He returns and asks Peter, 'Simon, are you asleep?' Shortly afterwards the betrayer arrives, Jesus is arrested and his friends run away in the dark of the night. In the courtyard of the high priest, when challenged, Peter denies even knowing Jesus; 'I don't know this man you're talking about!' (14:71)

When the crowds have the opportunity to release the man they hailed as the Messiah only days before, they listen to their religious leaders who 'had stirred up the crowd to have Pilate release Barabbas instead' (15:11). And they cry out, 'Crucify him!' When Jesus is brought to the place of execution, he is stripped naked and at 'the third hour they crucified him'. While hanging naked, to public view, Jesus is mocked and taunted.

Step by grim step, Jesus is stripped of everything. First a friend betrays him; then all his friends run away and leave him; his closest friend, Simon Peter, denies that he even knows him. Gradually Jesus sinks deeper and deeper into the black pit of dismal abandonment. The crowds reject him totally, choosing a murderer instead; he loses the last of his dignity when he is stripped in public and hung up to be mocked. Evil appears to have triumphed, as Mark suggests, when he says 'darkness came over the whole land until the ninth hour'. Then Jesus, feeling totally rejected and abandoned by everyone cries out:

'My God, my God, why have you forsaken me?' (15:34)

In his lonely death agony (Mark places no one at the foot of the cross apart from the soldiers), Jesus feels that even God has abandoned him. It is a dark lonely scene of utter desolation; he can sink no lower.

The dying words of Jesus, according to Mark, are a direct quotation from the opening words of Psalm 22. There is no space here to comment on them but a reading of the psalm reveals a disturbing prophecy, now tragically fulfilled.

Immediately after Jesus has died and he has done his Father's will, there is, at last, the first glimmer of faith and hope. And from an unexpected quarter. The Roman centurion (a despised Gentile) in charge of the executioners and the accompanying guard says,

'Surely this man was the Son of God!' (15:39)

It took a pagan to acknowledge Jesus as the Messiah, or, at the very least, a very special person worthy of respect. Halfway through the Gospel, at Caesarea Philippi, Jesus had asked, 'Who do people say I am?'; at the end, a Roman Gentile gives the answer.

Once again Mark has a message for his people, who are caught up in a similar downward spiral of violence and rejection. 'Hold on,' Mark is saying; 'have faith and trust in God, no matter how desperate things seem to be. Hang on, in faith, by your fingernails, if necessary. Jesus was there before you; he hung on in faith in God, even when things were so bad that he began to feel that God had abandoned him. Place all your faith and trust in God; all will be well; as it was with Jesus.'

On the third day, the tomb is found empty. To the women, who go to the tomb 'very early in the morning on the first day of the week . . . when the sun had risen', the white-robed messenger says, 'Don't be alarmed . . . He has risen!' The Son has risen. Here is the ultimate triumph and glory; God has rewarded Jesus for his total trust and abandonment to his will. Jesus is established as Christ and Lord of all.

You too will rise, Mark is saying to his people; you too will triumph, if you have the same faith and abandonment to the will of God as Jesus.

Questions for discussion

1. Why did Judas betray Jesus? Mark says it was for a sum of money, but that was only the equivalent of a labourer's wage for three months. Could there be some other, more compelling, reason?

2. Faced with the same hostility that Peter faced in the courtyard of the High Priest's house, would we have had the courage to admit that we were one of Jesus' friends? Do we even admit we are Christians to our neighbours and colleagues at work?

3. Why did none of his male followers, according to Mark, stay loyal to Jesus? Does it imply a lack of belief in him as the Messiah? Was their faith only skin-deep, or did they misread the signs and have the wrong expectations of Jesus as the Messiah?

4. The obedience of Jesus to his Father took him to the cross. Have you always believed that Jesus really and truly suffered great physical and mental pain? Or have you imagined that he was preserved from it by his relationship with God?

5. Mark's friends in the Roman community would have drawn much strength and encouragement from the way Mark recounts the Passion story. Can we benefit today in a similar way? Can our faith be deepened, if we understand the message Mark is trying to convey?

6. The empty tomb on Easter morning, and the announcement 'He is risen!' is all (if we accept the appearances were added later) Mark gives us on which to found our faith in the Resurrection. Is it enough?

Prayer

The ideal prayer here is the following one written by Charles de Foucauld the French missionary and founder of the Little Brothers of Jesus. Like Christ he died alone, in the Sahara, an apparent failure. The prayer must be said as though Christ himself was praying these words in and through us to his Father.

Father,
  I abandon myself into your hands;
  do with me what you will.
  Whatever you may do I thank you:
  I am ready for all, I accept all.

Let only your will be done in me,
  and in all your creatures.
  I wish no more than this, O Lord.

Into your hands I commend my soul:
  I offer it to you
  with all the love of my heart,
  for I love you, Lord,
  and so need to give myself,
  to surrender myself into your hands,
  without reserve,
  and with boundless confidence,
  for you are my Father.
Amen.